THE CANADIAN WEST
ALBERTA

Dawn, Foothills near Cowley

Overleaf: **Astotin Lake, Elk Island National Park**

THE CANADIAN WEST

ALBERTA

DOUGLAS LEIGHTON

ALTITUDE

Canadian Rockies/Vancouver

PUBLICATION INFORMATION

Canadian Cataloguing in Publication Data
Leighton, Douglas, 1953-
Alberta
Foothills ISBN 1-55153-118-6
Calgary ISBN 1-55153-119-4
Edmonton ISBN 1-55153-120-8
1. Alberta--Pictorial works. I. Title.
FC3662.L44 1995   971.23'04'0222   C95-911013-5
F1076.8.L44 1995

10 9 8 7 6 5 4

Edited by Faye Holt
Designed by Stephen Hutchings
Electronic page layout by Sandra Davis
Map by Cathering Burgess
(Base Map Copyright © 1995 Magellan Geographix)
Financial management by Laurie Smith

This book is dedicated to my parents, Joyce and Don, who were born and raised in Alberta.

Made in Western Canada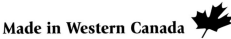
Printed and bound in Canada by Friesen Printers, Altona, Manitoba

Altitude Green Tree Program
Altitude Publishing will plant in Canada twice as many trees as were used in the manufacturing of this book.

Altitude Publishing Canada Ltd.
Canadian Rockies • Vancouver
1500 Railway Avenue, Canmore, Alberta T1W 1P6

Alberta Wild Rose

CONTENTS

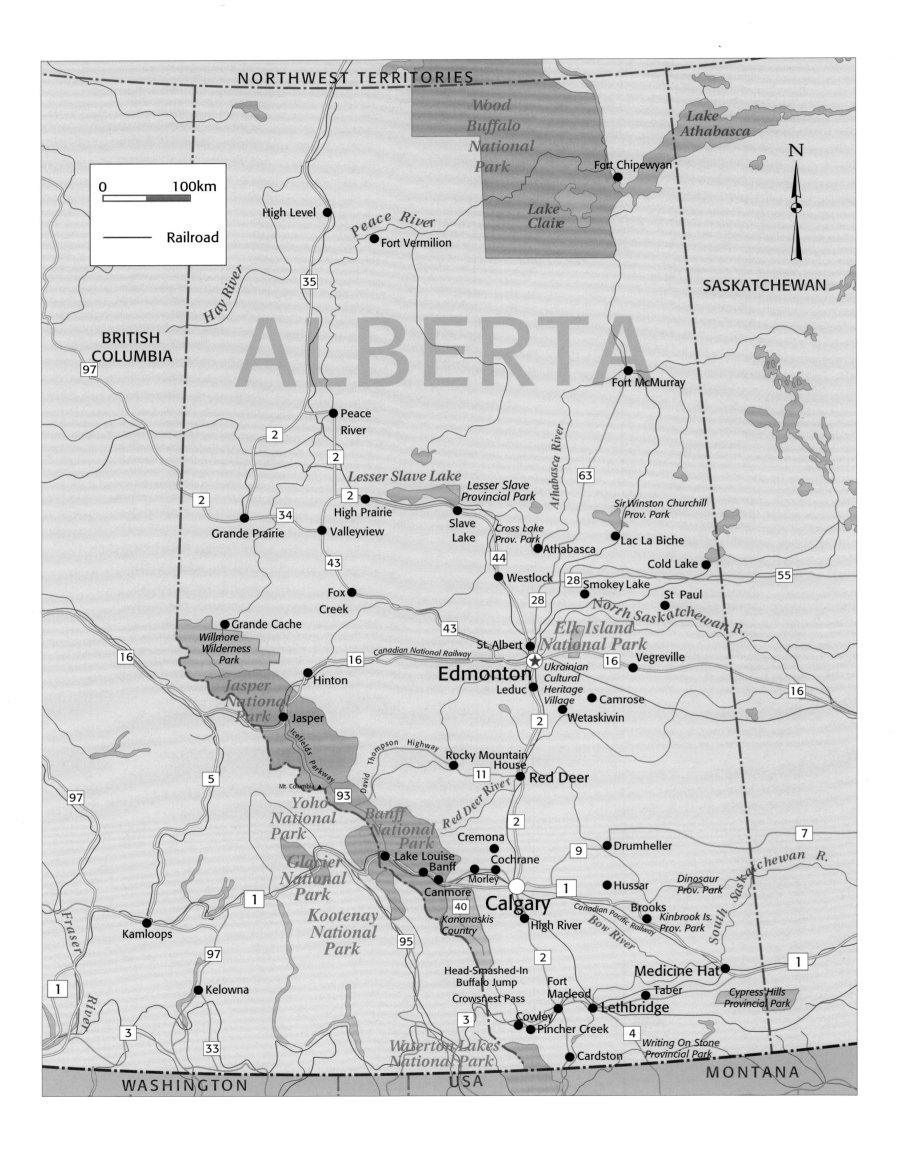

ALBERTA

I was lucky enough to be born in Alberta and feel luckier still to be an outdoor photographer in this area. What a wealth of material to work with! Within one province there's an exceptional diversity of landscapes. Each has its own natural and cultural communities: the Rocky Mountains with their rolling foothills; the prairies with their river badlands; the parklands with their aspen groves and farms; and the vast northern forests with their countless loon lakes and long summer sunsets.

About the only thing that Alberta doesn't have is a seacoast, but for most of its geological history, it did. That ancient history and its legacy of massive oil and natural gas deposits have everything to do with today's prosperous province.

Alberta became a province on September 1, 1905. Long before that it had been home to aboriginal peoples for countless generations. Then it became part of Canadian frontier history, following the northern rivers of the fur trade, chasing the bison of the Wild West, and then bringing civilization with the railroads. Apart from the international tourism already pouring into the Canadian Pacific Rockies, the new province anticipated a quiet, rural future. It would be built on rich farms and prime Alberta beef. Certainly, in parts of the province, that dream has held true.

But traces of oil had been found in the foothills as early as 1870, and in 1914 the first significant oil discovery in the British Empire was made at Turner Valley. Nearby Calgary was transformed into an oil company headquarters. From there the search was on and finally, in 1947, the patient drillers hit their first gusher at Leduc. Nearby Edmonton was a natural for the industry's operational centre. The benefits were neatly divided between Alberta's two major cities and spread out to wherever oil or natural gas were found—which seemed to be just about everywhere! This fossil legacy launched Alberta on a path to prosperity that the first pioneers could scarcely have imagined.

Today's Alberta has a brand new infrastructure and modern cities in a land where wide open spaces still beckon. Its population of over 2.6 million live in a province of 661,190 square kilometres. Seventy-five percent of Albertans live in major cities. Should they decide to get away from it all, the mountains, the country, and the lakes, are waiting. Within hours on a superb highway system, anyone can go from a digital urban environment to the trailheads of wilderness parks shaped only by nature. In between, all kinds of recreation invite enthusiasts. That's the true beauty of Alberta. The choice is yours.

Alberta's nickname of "Next Year Country" was born of fickle weather making early crops fail and was adopted later when oil rigs came up dry. The early pioneers were risk takers on a new land, and try as they might, all their dreams didn't come true. Still, there was always next year, and they looked forward to it. Optimism has always reigned in Alberta. With a province like this, who can doubt it?

DOUGLAS LEIGHTON

Previous pages: **Storm over Mt. Rundle, Vermilion Lakes, Banff National Park**

THE SOUTH

The Trans-Canada Highway in southern Alberta is a marvellous piece of engineering. Twinned and straight across level prairies and farmlands, it gets you there fast. You see ranches and farms, soaring hawks, and, in season, more gophers (Richardson's ground squirrels) than fenceposts. With luck, you glimpse pronghorn or deer. The big skies can be filled with spectacular clouds or astonishing sunsets. Still, it's not the scenic route and leaves a false impression.

Try turning north at Brooks and driving a half hour through lush, irrigated farmlands, past ponds rippled with ducks and hedgerows thick with pheasants. The dry grassland beyond them are flat as a table, or more accurately, flat as the bottom of the shallow lake was when the last Ice Age melted and the rich prairie soils were deposited. Then just when the land begins to lull you, it suddenly falls away to a stunning panorama of multi-coloured badlands and weird, wonderful hoodoos at the rim of the Red Deer River valley. It's Dinosaur Provincial Park, a mini-Grand Canyon world famous for its fabulous fossils.

Southern Alberta is that kind of place. It catches you by surprise with hidden beauties easily swallowed up in the vastness of this land. Green river valleys cut deeply across the plains, and the Cypress Hills south of Medicine Hat rise like a forested island above them. Turn south at Brooks, and there's big Lake Newell, with white sails and pelicans gliding over its surface. There are

Plains Bison, Waterton Lakes National Park

Left: **Red Rock Canyon, Waterton Lakes National Park**

1 1

swaths of bright green corn, golden wheat, yellow canola, and blue flax. Then there is the subtle beauty and unique wildlife of native grasslands. In the west, these grasslands climb the foothills and come to a stunning conclusion at Waterton Lakes in the southern Rockies, one of Canada's most overlooked national parks.

While driving across these vast prairies at 100 kilometres an hour, try imagining what life must have been like for the prehistoric peoples here—before they had horses. They faced ornery bull bison and prairie fires *on foot.* Horses, traded northward from their Spanish origins in the American Southwest, arrived in about 1725 and revolutionized the lives of the Blackfoot people as profoundly as the automobile changed our lives—suddenly people could run with the bison. Horses carried food, shelter, and the new iron tools—including firearms—obtained from neighbouring tribes long before they met the Europeans who made them.

When the 1857–60 British Palliser Expedition came west to survey the potential of the lands along the new international boundary, they wrote off south-eastern Alberta and adjacent Saskatchewan, named the Palliser's Triangle, as a useless desert—leaving it as the last stronghold of the bison and the Blackfoot. Yet, only a decade later the bison were disappearing and big trouble was brewing with the Sioux tribes south of the border and threatening to spread north. Inflaming everything, Montana whisky traders were selling their firewater from Fort Whoop-Up (near Lethbridge). But by the time tensions exploded at the bloody Little Bighorn in 1876, all was quiet on the Canadian front. With the arrival of the North West Mounted Police, Alberta's Wild West was not won, but it was negotiated.

In the fall of 1874 the red-coated Mounties rode in and began building forts. Fort Macleod, in the heart of Blackfoot country, was the first and main garrison. Within months, the NWMP chased out the bootleggers and established a sense of law and order. Most importantly, the Mounties were men of their word, and their British Empire justice was fair and colour-blind, something Blackfoot Chief Crowfoot was quick to note. Knowing

the bison were gone for good and inspired by a vision of the future, this wise "statesmen in paint and blanket" signed Treaty No. 7 in 1877. It created some of the largest native reserves in Canada and set the stage for peaceful settlement.

As Waterton pioneer Kootenai Brown observed, "where buffalo thrived, cattle will do the same." Not surprisingly, the boundless, empty grasslands caught the eyes of ranchers. Then in 1883 the Canadian Pacific Railway raced—at up to 14.5 kilometres (9 miles) per day!—across the southern prairies. The isolated plains were suddenly right on the transnational highway. Medicine Hat was born that year, and natural gas found by workers drilling for water soon fueled industries. By 1921 Medalta Stoneware shipped east the first manufactured goods from Alberta. Rails reached the coal mines of Lethbridge in 1885 and crossed the Crowsnest Pass in 1898. In 1887 Mormon settlers from Utah established Cardston. Initiating Alberta's first irrigation project, they showed how fertile the land could be. Large scale irrigation began at Lethbridge in 1900 and then Brooks in 1910.

Pioneer Kootenai Brown saw more than just grass for cattle in the foothills. Seeing the beauty of Waterton Lakes and the changes that threatened it, he became the driving force behind the eventual establishment of the park. With similar foresight, the government established provincial parks in the most beautiful and significant areas of the south.

Every small town has its proud museum, but in the 1980s this tradition took a world class turn with the building of the Royal Tyrrell Museum of Paleontology at Drumheller, the Remington Alberta Carriage Centre in Cardston, as well as interpretive centres at the Frank Slide in the Crowsnest Pass and Head-Smashed-In Buffalo Jump near Fort Macleod.

There are beautiful places in the heart of Canada's Wild West. Even though Alberta is not just cowboy country, cowboys are still riding here, herding cattle "where the deer and the antelope play."

Right: **Native Dancer**

Frank Slide Interpretive Centre, Crowsnest Pass

In the early morning of April 29, 1903, 82 million tonnes of Turtle Mountain slid down and covered three square kilometres of land in less than 100 seconds. Most of the coal mining town of Frank was buried by up to 30 metres of limestone rubble. The miraculous escapes and other stories are illustrated at the hilltop visitor centre.

Previous Pages: **Waterton Lakes, Waterton Townsite, Waterton Lakes National Park**

A forest reserve since 1895, a National Park since 1911, and an International Peace Park since 1932, this park is tucked into the far southwestern corner of Alberta. Here boat tours cruise down the lake to Glacier National Park in Montana during the summer months. Since 1927 the Prince of Wales Hotel on the isthmus between upper and lower Waterton Lakes has been buffeted by the valley's famous winds.

Wheatfields, Foothills, Rockies near Cardston

Some of the best wheat in the world is grown in Alberta. Most of the foothills are used for ranching, but where soils are suitable, the moisture spilling over the Rockies can produce bumper crops.

Musical Ride at Fort Macleod Museum

At this re-creation of the 1874 North West Mounted Police fort, the first in Alberta, these unofficial summer Mounties exhibit their horsemanship for visitors. The scarlet uniforms—in the British Imperial tradition—impressed the Blackfoot people here, as did the character of those wearing them, leading to a peaceful settlement of the prairies.

Head-Smashed-In Buffalo Jump near Fort Macleod

Used for at least 5700 years, this low, 300-metre-long cliff at the foot of the Porcupine Hills is almost invisible from the slopes above it, making it ideal for stampeding bison over it to their deaths. The site is named for an unfortunate young Blackfoot hunter who wondered what a jumping buffalo would look like from below the cliff! A fascinating visitor centre, built into the cliff, tells the story of Blackfoot bison culture at this World Heritage Site.

Alberta Beef, Beaver Valley, Porcupine Hills

Spring storms bring even greener pastures for cattle grazing these foothills north of Pincher Creek. The Piegans saw a resemblance between these hills, studded with pine and Douglas fir, and the porcupines providing quills for both tools and decorations.

Nikka Yuko Japanese Gardens, Lethbridge.

Built as a 1967 Canadian centennial project, this 1.6 hectare enclave within Henderson Park features an authentic Japanese garden and pavilion where "Beauty in Simplicity" is revealed in the placement of every manicured tree, shrub, and stone.

Writing on Stone

Protected in an archaeological reserve within Writing-on-Stone Provincial Park is the largest concentration of native rock carvings, or petroglyphs, on the North American plains. These shield-bearing warriors as well as hunters on horseback, bison, bighorn sheep, and bears are carved into the sandstone. Guided summer tours also explore the hoodoos.

Right: **Writing-on-Stone Provincial Park**

Weird sandstone formations along the Milk River made this a sacred place for the Blackfoot people. Even today some campers find it spooky or spiritual when, on a moonlit night, coyote howls ignite imaginations and these glowing hoodoos seem to become supernatural forms. The Milk River is the only Alberta drainage that flows south into the Mississippi River basin. The distant Sweetgrass Hills, in Montana, were used as a lookout for these bison-hunting people.

Cliff Swallows, Bow River north of Taber

With the young of the year out practising their maneuvres, the whole colony of cliff swallows takes wing over the water, getting ready to leave their city of gourd-like mud nests under this bridge for another year. Water, through vast irrigation systems, turns much of the prairies to green in a region which grows sweet Taber corn, sugar beets, and other produce.

Right: **Plains Prickly Pear Cactus Flowers**

Every June the driest prairies, riverbanks, and badlands in southeastern Alberta are punctuated with these big "yellow roses" and the smaller pink blooms of the pincushion cactus. Surprisingly, these pears were harvested by native peoples who burned off the spines and ate the fleshy fruit inside.

Medicine Hat, South Saskatchewan River Valley

This oasis in the hottest, driest part of Alberta began as a Canadian Pacific Railway camp in 1883 and is now a prosperous city of 45,000. Rising on the horizon above the city of shady, green streets and red brick buildings are the Cypress Hills, dusted with a late spring snow.

Horseshoe Canyon, Cypress Hills Provincial Park

The hills rise 450 metres above the surrounding prairies to the elevation of the mountain town of Banff. Called the "Thunder Breeding Hills" by the Blackfoot people, here the lush forest attests to the moister climate. Most of the hills are within the 200 square kilometres of Alberta's second largest provincial park. The ski hill, lakes, and holiday hamlet of Elkwater make it an ideal escape for the residents of nearby Medicine Hat.

Lake Newell, Kinbrook Island Provincial Park

Surrounded by sun-baked, shortgrass prairie south of Brooks, this lake is one of many reservoirs created as part of the region's irrigation system. Beginning in 1910, water turned near desert to lush farms and gardens, provided cool summer splashes for sailors and swimmers, and created rich new habitat for the cormorants and pelicans that fish here.

Left: **Pronghorn Buck**

Though usually called antelope, the pronghorn is the only survivor of a unique North American mammal subfamily. Superbly adapted for prairie life, his huge eyes see for miles. With lightning speed—and bursts of up to 60 kilometres per hour—the fastest North American animal can easily escape predators. Once more numerous than bison, pronghorn neared extinction in 1900 but are now doing well on the southeastern rangelands where they browse sage and shrubs beside the cattle grazing grass. Deep winter snow is their deadliest enemy.

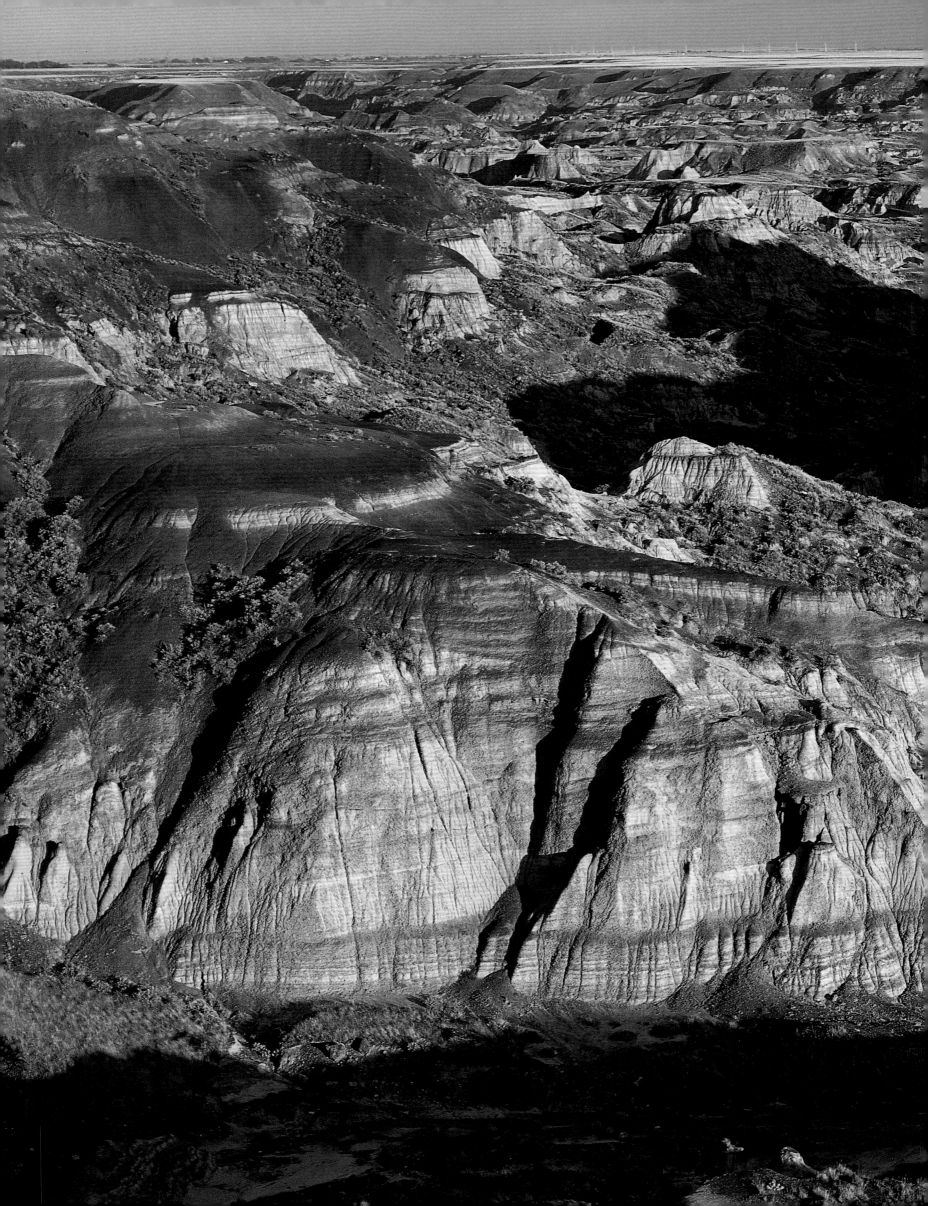

Moonrise, Badlands, Dinosaur Provincial Park

A fantastic landscape has been sculpted out of a layer of bentonite, exposing the ancient deposit and its dinosaur bones to river, rain, and wind erosion.

Left: **Ornithomimus Fossil, Dinosaur Provincial Park**

Freshly unearthed by Dr. Phil Currie of the Royal Tyrrell Museum of Paleontology, this superbly intact fossil is among the best specimens of these bird-mimic dinosaurs yet discovered.

Previous pages: **Dinosaur Provincial Park**

Declared a United Nations World Heritage Site in 1979, the eroded badlands along the Red Deer River north of Brooks hold one of the greatest known deposits of dinosaur fossils in the world.

Trail Ride, Red Deer River Valley near Drumheller

Albertans love their cowboy image. Many still ride as working cowboys on ranches, and weekend cowboys find plenty of room to play. Trail rides are part of many Alberta vacations.

Right: **Albertosaurus, Royal Tyrrell Museum of Paleontology**

Opened in 1985 in the badlands of the Red Deer River valley near Drumheller, this state-of-the-art museum displays the 3.6 billion year history of life. The Albertosaurus was a smaller—yet still 10 metre long—and more nimble cousin of the famous Tyrannosaurus Rex. Terrorizing the herds of duckbilled dinosaurs that roamed the lush coastal deltas here 75 million years ago, it was first discovered in the area in 1884 by geologist Joseph B. Tyrrell.

Rainbow near Cochrane

Rolling prairie west of Calgary was the site of the 40,500 hectare Cochrane Ranch, one of the first big ranches in the Alberta foothills.

Left: **Canola Field, Grain Elevators at Hussar**

Although it looks like the field was planted for the benefit of sightseers, these lemon-yellow blossoms are canola, the crop of the 90s. A long genetic leap from their rapeseed ancestry, these seeds yield oil with the healthy distinction of having the lowest level of saturated fat for any vegetable oil.

CALGARY AND BANFF

Calgary, with a population of over 750,000 and climbing, is Canada's sixth largest metropolitan area, yet ranks a close third in its number of corporate head offices. Most of these are directly related to the oil and natural gas industries, but increasing numbers are not. In an era when office location is becoming more a matter of choice, many organizations are choosing Calgary. Ask their executives why, and they'll respond with all of the sound business reasons—Canada's youngest and best educated work force, high-tech state-of-the-art infrastructure, an international airport receiving a facility ranking of third in the world in 1995, and a spacious, vibrant, livable city—then pause to glance out their office windows at the snowcapped Rockies, an easy hour away, with the kinds of expressions that obviate further explanation.

Calgarians enjoy the good life here, blessed with an enticing array of options. To ski, or not to ski? To go cycling, golfing, sailing, or flycasting for big rainbow trout in the Bow River DOWNTOWN after work? Dinner in the mountains or an afternoon at the zoo or Heritage Park? An amateur rodeo, or a world class equestrian event at Spruce Meadows? There are summer and winter festivals, country and classical concerts, Broadway shows, gallery openings, and hockey games. Throw in the Calgary Stampede, when everybody gets to be a cowboy or cowgirl and let loose for a week, and it becomes clear that Calgarians have the opportunity to play as hard as they work.

Sunrise on Calgary Skyline

Left: **Calgary Towers**

Looking at the glass towers of downtown Calgary today, one has difficulty believing that this humming, modern metropolis is only six generations old. Its natural setting, the sheltered, wooded Bow River valley at the foot of the Rocky Mountain foothills, had made an ideal campsite for aboriginal peoples, who had first driven bison over riverbank jumps here 8,000 years ago. In 1875 this was Sarcee (allies of the Blackfoot) territory, when 50 men of the North West Mounted Police rode in to its isolated valley and established Fort Calgary. Treaties were signed in 1877 (part of Calgary is leased Sarcee land) and soon sprawling ranches, often created by British officers "retiring in the colonies," were taking shape in the foothills. In 1881 the first big herd of cattle was driven up to Cochrane, just west of the fort, Calgary's future looked like that of nearby High River (a prosperous ranching centre, population 6000) today.

Then, in 1883, the Canadian Pacific Railway abruptly steamed into town and up the Bow Valley to the Rockies. Calgary became the railway's western operations centre, a base camp for the subsequent assault on the western mountains, and a full-fledged "Cow Town" shipping cattle to the east. More importantly, as it turned out, it became the world's gateway to the Canadian Rockies.

Railway manager William Van Horne was a pragmatic visionary, always searching for ways to generate revenue. When he first saw the Rockies, he knew immediately what their most valuable resource was: absolutely stunning beauty, the kind that people all over the world would come to see. When he heard that hot springs had been discovered just off the line, he knew that they could rival the famous spas of the Swiss Alps. The Canadian government, deep in railway debt, heartily agreed; and in 1885 the land immediately around the Banff hot springs was reserved for Canada's first national park, established in 1887 as Rocky Mountains National Park.

The next year the first Banff Springs Hotel, an oasis of luxury in the wilderness, opened for the summer; followed by the first log chalet at Lake Louise in 1890. Advertised worldwide as a key attraction on the CPR's "Europe-to-the-Orient" rail and steamship route, the Rockies were soon teeming with Victorian adventurers, tourists, and visiting dignitaries. Mountaineers raced to make initial ascents of whole new ranges of summits, and by 1899 the CPR had Swiss guides leading guests to the peaks. Most visitors, however, toured the sights around Banff and Lake Louise by train, buggy, or boat—automobiles did not arrive until 1910—and soaked in the "medicinal" hot springs water. The "Canadian Pacific Rockies," as the company advertised them, have been a world famous recreation destination ever since.

In the 1970s, with the Calgary oil industry booming, unprecedented numbers of happy campers were overcrowding into Banff; and the Alberta government decided to create an alternative destination for them. Kananaskis Country is a spectacular 5,200 square kilometre mountain playground in the Rockies south of Banff National Park. It encompasses three parks—including Peter Lougheed Provincial Park, a 508 square kilometre jewel—and a whole spectrum of first class recreational facilities in and around them. Kananaskis Village was born with three hotels, complemented by an adjacent superb golf course, and a brand new ski area at Nakiska built to host the downhill events of the 1988 Winter Olympics. Concurrently, near the then somnolent little town of Canmore, the Nordic Centre and its environs were developed to meet the requirements of the cross country skiing and related events of those same Olympics. When the world arrived to witness that grand spectacle, they discovered that this area had "arrived" as well. That snowball is still rolling...

Today, many international visitors plan their holidays to be here in July for the region's biggest double feature: the Calgary Stampede, the "Greatest Outdoor Show on Earth," then the Rockies, the "Greatest Outdoors on Earth." The drive in between may well remind them of other features that they've seen—at the movies. Filming some of the best recent "Westerns" here, Hollywood has discovered the area too. It has all the services she needs and her stars demand, and settings that still look as wild and beautiful as those of the old "Wild West." Indeed, the cowboys and Indians are still here - but now they're packing cell phones.

Right: **Stephen Avenue Mall, Downtown Calgary**

Ski Jump Towers, Canada Olympic Park

Standing on the west edge of the city, these ski jumping towers are conspicuous reminders of the 1988 Winter Olympics. Here also are the luge and bobsleigh tracks, where those events were held, and the Olympic Hall of Fame.

Right: **Sunset, Calgary Skyline with Canadian Airlines Saddledome**

The Saddledome, another Olympic legacy, is the home of the National Hockey League Calgary Flames and now rivals the Calgary Tower as the city's best known landmark.

Saddle Bronc Rider, Calgary Stampede

For eight long seconds this cowboy holds on with one hand, while his ornery mount, bred to buck, does its best to eject him. At the first Stampede, in 1912, Alberta Blood native Tom Three Persons won this event with his legendary ride on Cyclone, a nasty black bronco which had bucked off all cowboys before him. This kind of action happens every summer weekend in rodeos big and small across Alberta.

Rangeland Derby, Calgary Stampede

In the signature event of the annual Greatest Outdoor Show on Earth, chuckwagon teams of racing thoroughbreds, canny drivers, and mud-splattered outriders thunder around the track in pursuit of big bucks and prestige. Based on the cooks' chuckwagons, which fed the trail driving cowboys, these sophisticated wagons would never be late for lunch.

Glass and Steel, Downtown Calgary

Most of downtown Calgary, with all its modern conveniences, has been built in the last three decades. On those winter days when the chinook winds fail to warm the city, downtown shoppers and workers can still walk between buildings in the street-spanning Plus 15 connectors.

Right: **Edmontosaurus, Calgary Zoo**

Recognized as one of the finest zoos on the continent, the Calgary Zoo features living species in spacious, hospitable habitats and displays life-size models of dinosaurs in its Prehistoric Park. Herds of these duckbilled dinosaurs were once common in coastal Alberta 75 million years ago.

Rocky Mountaineer Passenger Train, Bow Valley near Canmore

As they have since 1885, train passengers marvel at the views from the Canadian Pacific Railway line through the Rockies. This independently operated Calgary to Vancouver touring train has been continuing that tradition since 1990.

Left: **Barrier Lake, Kananaskis Country**

Just off the Trans-Canada Highway west of Calgary, a glacial blue reservoir along Highway 40 is the first grand view welcoming visitors to Kananaskis or K-Country. The new mountain playground offers recreation ranging from wilderness camping to campgrounds with cable. Visitors also enjoy luxury hotels, a world-renowned golf course, cycling, hiking, equestrian trails, and ski areas. Summer sightseers can drive over Highwood Pass, the highest highway in Canada.

Previous Pages: **McDougall Memorial Church, Morley**

Standing above the north bank of the Bow River since 1875, this historic church has witnessed an astonishing transformation in the land and lives around it.

Rainbow over Town of Banff, Banff National Park

As a spring storm from the prairies meets the sun setting over the Continental Divide, a rainbow glows above the town of Banff and its historic icon, the Banff Springs Hotel.

Left: **Three Sisters Peaks near Canmore**

These landmark peaks—the highest is 2936 metres—were named for their resemblance, when dusted with snow, to three nuns. Coal was mined at their base until the 1960s, but now the once sleepy town of Canmore has become a thriving recreation and service centre, a new gateway to both Banff and Kananaskis Country.

Sunset over Castle Mountain, Bow River, Banff National Park

This best-named peak in the Rockies stands above the Bow Valley, its highest tower rising to 2766 metres. At the junction with Vermilion Pass, leading west across the Continental Divide, it has long been a familiar landmark for travellers.

Left: **Sunrise over Vermilion Lakes, Banff National Park**

Mt. Rundle, emerging from the rising autumn mists, was named for Wesleyan missionary Reverend Robert Rundle, who met the Stoney people here in 1847. He climbed a nearby mountain but not the 2949 metre peak that bears his name.

Lower Falls, Johnson's Canyon, Banff National Park

Ashort walk along a canyon walkway from the Bow Valley Parkway leads to these falls and others further up. Shady and bathed in cool mist, the canyon is a retreat on a hot summer day. This is also a mecca for bird-watchers searching for Black Swifts, mountain aerialists that soar high among the peaks feeding on insects and nest on the canyon walls here.

Right: **Moraine Lake, Banff National Park**

Wow! That's the universal exclamation of visitors here, walking up the rockpile for which the lake is named and finding the famous view unfold before them. This scene became a Canadian icon when its image was placed on the back of the $20 bill—when $20 was worth something!

Chateau Lake Louise, Lake Louise Ski Area, Banff National Park

Sitting on the shore of frozen Lake Louise, the first two wings of this historic Canadian Pacific Railway hotel were opened in 1928 on a site occupied by rough chalets since 1890. The third wing was completed, and the entire hotel lavishly renovated in 1988. The lights of snow-grooming machines twinkle across the Bow Valley at Ski Louise, one of the largest downhill ski areas in Canada.

Right: **Lake Louise**

After recovering from the shock of walking into the most beautiful postcard in the Rockies, many summer visitors take time to experience the real Lake Louise, canoeing its calm waters, exploring its shoreline trails, taking a hike or trail ride to an alpine teahouse, or even climbing the ice-capped 3464 metre summit of Mt. Victoria. Others apparently never do get over the shock, content to simply sit, sun, and stare.

Farm Fields near Cremona

These freshly plowed fields reveal the richness of some foothills soils. Not all black gold is oil.

Right: **Cronquist House, Red Deer**

Overlooking Bower Ponds in the city's riverside Waskasoo Park, this Victorian farmhouse was built in 1911 and moved here in 1976. Today it serves as the city's multicultural centre and a beautiful reminder of the past.

Previous Pages: **Peyto Lake, Banff National Park**

Looking north from 2069 metre Bow Summit down the Mistaya Valley, this panorama offers travellers a mountaineer's view just a short walk from the Icefields Parkway.

EDMONTON AND JASPER

Twenty-five kilometres west of Jasper, the Yellow-head Pass is the lowest and easiest pass across the Canadian Rockies. It was a natural route for aboriginal peoples long before fur traders started using it in the early 1800s. In 1872, when surveyors came looking for a route for the promised transcontinental Canadian railway, the Yellowhead was recommended because of the pass and the rich farm and timber lands along this northern route. In the path was Fort Edmonton. A strategic trading post since 1795, the community fully expected to become the railway capital—until 1883 when the Canadian Pacific Railway finally arrived but on a southern line through Calgary!

Despite this blow, Edmonton kept growing. The area had natural advantages. On the North Saskatchewan River, the riverbanks were full of coal. Surrounded by rich, well-watered potential farmlands, the vicinity kept attracting settlers, especially after a rail branch line arrived. Business boomed when the 1890s Klondike Gold Rush roared through on its way north. Then in 1905 Alberta became a province and, despite fierce opposition from Calgary, Edmonton was named the capital. As a result, Alberta was destined to have two great cities, sibling rivals forever arguing over which had the best weather and culture, but especially which had the best sports teams. Much to Calgary's dismay, in the 1980s Edmonton's National Hockey League Oilers, led by superstar Wayne Gretzy at his

Oil Well, Northern Lights, East of Edmonton

Left: **Sunset over Edmonton Skyline**

best, and Canadian Football League Edmonton Eskimos went on such a winning streak that the city officially dubbed itself the "City of Champions."

Historically, Edmonton is better known as the Gateway to the North, a fitting description since the days of the Klondike prospectors (though Fort Edmonton had also been a gateway to the west.) This gate got busier as aircraft opened up the north, and it swung wide open to build the Alaska Highway during World War Two. The city grew supplying and servicing northern frontier development, and it celebrates this historic role every July during Klondike Days, 10 days of rollicking entertainment and events.

The city itself mirrors the huge north in its urban vastness. Edmonton sprawls over 679 square kilometres making it larger than Toronto, which has more than four times Edmonton's 850,000 population. All this space allows the residents more parkland per capita than any other North American city. Included is most of the lushly forested North Saskatchewan River valley, which winds through the city centre. There's room here for Fort Edmonton Park, Canada's largest historic park, the Valley Zoo, the pyramids of the Muttart Conservancy, the John Janzen Nature Centre, three golf courses, riverside paths, cycling and cross-country ski trails, and a ski hill used in summer for outdoor events. Still there are plenty of natural areas for wildlife. And in West Edmonton, there's room for the world's largest shopping mall and entertainment park.

In the huge expanses of the north, meetings were a cause for celebration. That spirit lives in the Festival City's many summer gatherings: Klondike Days, the multicultural Heritage Days, Fringe Theatre Festival, Folk Music Festival, Street Performers' Festival, International Children's Festival, First Nations' Dreamspeakers Festival, a Caribbean Mardi Gras Carnival, Visual Arts Celebration, and more.

North of the Chinook belt, the snow stays, and winter feels like winter. Skiers love the river valley ski hill and cross-country trails. Birdwatchers ignore the cold and join in the largest Christmas bird count on the continent. Maybe it's those long winter nights that give Edmonton such a vibrant artistic and cultural community, where so many seem to have the energy to create art, drama, and music and so many others take the time to enjoy it. Edmonton's great indoors also include Broadway shows, rock concerts, Imax films at the Space and Science Centre, art galleries, the provincial museum, and various archives. Both indoors and outdoors, the architectural details of the 1912 legislature building are impressive.

The same year that Edmonton became the capital, the long awaited railway finally arrived. Heading west through the Yellowhead, it brought a flood of Ukrainian, French, German, Polish, and Scandinavian farmers to the area. Looking south to the success of the CPR's national parks tourism, the railway builders pushed for the same on their line through the Rockies. Here again there were hot springs, spectacular scenery, plus Maligne Lake, the largest lake in the Rockies, the Columbia Icefields, the largest icecap south of the Arctic and at 3747 metres, Mt. Columbia, Alberta's highest peak. Just over Yellowhead Pass soared another superlative attraction, 3954 metre Mt. Robson, the highest peak in the Canadian Rockies. In sharp contrast to these icy summits, the lower Athabasca Valley was wide, warm, and speckled with refreshing lakes.

In 1907 the Jasper Forest Park was established and later became Jasper National Park. Jasper townsite, near an old trading post at the confluence of the Miette and Athabasca Rivers, started as a railway and tourist town called Fitzhugh—though at first it hosted few visitors. It took the Canadian National Railway until 1922 to complete its centrepiece near town, the Jasper Park Lodge, a country club in the wilderness. Today Jasper National Park has become the famous attraction those railway men envisioned.

Right: **Provincial Legislature Building, Edmonton**

Rice Howard Way, Downtown Edmonton

In 1995, this people place gained a new landmark, The Big Rock. The creation of city sculptors Catherine Burgess and Sandra Bromley, it stands in a busy square. Art, culture, and festivals galore give outlet to Edmonton's lively creative community.

Right: **Edmonton, North Saskatchewan River Valley**

Modern Edmonton loves its river valley, with its parks, playgrounds, natural areas, and cycling paths. The river has been the heart of the city since it was the fur trader's highway from Fort Edmonton to the distant world. Now prominent above the river is the baronial MacDonald Hotel and the pink convention centre.

Capital City Park

Flowers and manicured lawns are just part of 7400 hectares of parklands and recreational facilities—including a nature centre, a huge historic park, golf courses, ski areas, and riverside picnic spots—stretching along both sides of the river valley. Edmonton has more parkland per capita then any other Canadian city.

Columbus Discovers the West Edmonton Mall

Edmonton began as a trading post, and this enormous mall—still the largest in the world—follows that tradition in fantastic style. There's a world of shopping and dining in its 800 stores and services. Then there's this theme park with its exact replica of Christopher Columbus's Santa Maria, submarine rides, dolphins, skating rink, wave pool, state-of-the-thrill midway, and Fantasyland Hotel.

Ukrainian Cultural Heritage Village

Fifty kilometres east of Edmonton on the Yellowhead Highway (16), this recreated village celebrates the lives and culture of one of the major ethnic groups settling here between 1892 and 1930. Costumed actors depict traditional farm and town life in daily performances held during the summer.

Left: **Fort Edmonton**

In Edmonton's river valley is Fort Edmonton Park, which recreates not only the 1846 Hudson's Bay Company fur trading fort but the entire early history of the city in a series of period streets: the 1895 settlement, the 1905 new capital and the 1920s community. Antique cars, a streetcar, a steam train, and wagons provide equally diverse ways to explore the big park.

Storm, Astotin Lake, Elk Island National Park

A thunderstorm approaches the largest lake on this 194 square kilometre island of natural parklands just east of Edmonton. There's a beach, golf course, and campground, but most summer visitors come to view wildlife, including both plains and wood bison, elk, moose, deer and about 2000 beavers. With over 80 kilometres of cross-country ski trails, the park gets busier still in winter.

Right: **Mt. Athabasca, Sunwapta River, Jasper National Park**

This spectacular view awaits travellers on the Icefields Parkway. The 3491 metre peak is one in a ring of giants surrounding the 300 square kilometre Columbia Icefield on the spine of the Rockies. Another in the ring is Alberta's highest peak, 3747 metre Mt. Columbia. Athabasca Glacier, the source of this river, is the most accessible of the eight major glaciers fed by the icefield. Unique snow coaches transport many visitors to explore it.

Jasper Park Lodge, Jasper National Park

Sprawling on the shoreline of azure Lac Beauvert near the town of Jasper, this cottage-style lodge with its world famous golf course first opened in 1922 as the centrepiece in the Canadian National Railway's tourism development.

Left: **Dawn, Mt. Edith Cavell, Jasper National Park**

Towering far above its neighbours, the 3363 metre peak catches the first warm light of dawn and is reflected in the outlet of Lake Cavell below it. Hikers pass this spectacular view at the trailhead for Tonquin Valley, in the wilderness heart of the park. Others admire the peak from the town of Jasper.

Bull Wapiti, Talbot Lake, Jasper National Park

Elk, or wapiti, are the most common large mammal in the Rockies and find prime habitat and critical winter range in the dry montane forests of Jasper's lower Athabasca River valley. Here, a bull feeds on nutritious lakeshore greens to nourish his new set of antlers, still growing under velvet.

Right: **Maligne Lake, Jasper National Park**

Maligne is the largest lake in the Canadian Rockies. This spectacular view of Spirit Island at Sampson's Narrows midway down the lake is enjoyed by today's visitors from the comfort of modern tour boats. The boats are a far cry from the rough rafts built by Mary Schaffer's party, the first to explore the lake in 1908.

THE NORTH

I
f one calls southern Alberta "Canada's Texas" and the Rockies "Canada's Alps," then northern Alberta must surely be Canada's "Canada." Here is the land of the birchbark canoe and the early fur trade—the image of Canada the world knows. This is the land of vast forests and muskegs, huge lakes and rivers, caribou and beaver, loons calling, wolves howling, and Aurora Borealis shimmering in the northern sky.

Two-thirds of Alberta lies north of Edmonton. To the east, agricultural lands push about 200 kilometres farther north. In the west, the parklands—turned farmlands along the Peace and Hay Rivers—are among the most northerly agricultural lands in the world. Where soils are fertile, long summer days and abundant moisture compensate for the shortness of the growing season, and crops can be bountiful.

The rest is the North Woods, part of the great boreal forest that runs across Canada and Eurasia. The soils and climate are suited only to raising spruce and moose. Here lies most of Alberta's 16,800 square kilometres of fresh water. Lesser Slave Lake is the largest lake within the province; and huge Lake Athabasca, the lowest point in Alberta, is on the northeastern border.

Indeed, water is everywhere in the north. The mostly flat land soaks up the long winter's snowpack and the distant Rocky Mountain meltwaters carried by the Peace and Athabasca Rivers. Here is a canoeist's dream, pooled in the countless sparkling lakes and rivers that irrigate the lush boreal forests. But the north is also muskeg, quaking carpets of moss, and scraggly trees

Winter Forest south of Grande Prairie

Left: **Sunset, Buffalo Bay, Lesser Slave Lake**

floating like wet sponges on flooded ground. These were the greatest barriers to travel in the north. A broad band of muskeg between Grande Prairie and Edmonton delayed settlement of the fertile Peace River parklands for years. Stories of heavy equipment disappearing into apparently bottomless muskeg are part of northern legend and are fact. Still today, many resource workers must wait for freeze up before starting work in the bush.

Fortunately, vast muskegs, as well as luck, saved two of the conservation movement's most famous symbols—the whooping crane and the wood bison. Their safe haven is Canada's biggest but least famous national park. In 1894 the last wild bison, about 250–500 head, still survived on a remote island of parkland habitat in extreme northeastern Alberta. That year, legislation was enacted to protect them, enforced by the North West Mounted Police (thus the prominent bison on their insignia). In 1922 Wood Buffalo Park, an area of 44,800 square kilometres, was established to further protect the growing herd. By chance, this Switzerland-sized park also protected the last breeding habitat of the whooping crane. Discovered from the air in the 1950s, these nesting grounds and the Peace-Athabasca delta are two of the most important waterfowl habitats on the continent.

When you're "Up North," there's always a profound sense of vastness, a feeling that you're on the last frontier—and you are. Yet this last frontier was Alberta's first frontier. More than two centuries ago, Peter Pond of the North West Company found a bonanza of furs here. He founded Alberta's first European settlement, Fort Chipewyan on Lake Athabasca in 1778. From this westernmost post on their canoe route from Montreal, Alexander Mackenzie searched for a route to the Pacific. First he wrongly followed the Mackenzie River to the Arctic Ocean in 1789. Then he went up the Peace River and overland, achieving his goal—the first European crossing of the continent—by 1793. Soon rival traders from the Hudson Bay Company followed. The fur rush was on, with the competing companies establishing trading post as far south as Edmonton and Rocky Mountain House. Both the traders and their native partners prospered, setting the tone for future relationships, while the beaver lasted. When they were quickly depleted, Alberta's first boom was ended.

Railways, paddlewheelers and the first rough roads brought settlers until farmers and ranchers pushed to the edge of the forest. There the Chipewyan and Slave people, joined by the Cree and Metis who had moved here with the fur trade, still trapped, hunted, and fished. Many lived in the new trading post settlements, others in more remote traditional villages.

Then one day in the late 1920s, a new bird appeared in the sky. The airplane—more precisely "bushplanes" with summer floats and winter skis—opened up the north. Flown by courageous bush pilots who were skilled at everything from emergency landings in howling blizzards to makeshift engine repairs, these aircraft made it possible to get almost anywhere easily. They provided a life line to the scattered communities and a bird's eye view of this unknown land and its potential.

Prospectors, oilmen, and doctors followed. And so did adventurers, especially big game hunters and fishermen, who were soon staying at fly-in lodges built for them. Change came dramatically again with the oil boom of the 1970s. There was a rush of exploration and discoveries as well as the acceleration of the huge Athabasca oil sands projects near Fort McMurray. In the 1980s came huge forestry developments.

Now, though serviced by aircraft, penetrated by a few highways and ever more bush roads, most of this vast land still looks, feels, and sounds much as it did in the fur trading days. And that, in today's crowded world, may be its most precious resource of all.

Muskoseepi Park, Grande Prairie

Beautifully developed in 1986, Muskoseepi—Cree for "Bear Creek"—
Park is a 400 hectare green belt running through a booming, young city of
30,000. Long a quiet farming centre for the big prairie around it, the community has grown explosively in recent years with the expansion of the forest industry and the discovery of enormous local natural gas reserves.

Town of Peace River

Named for the peace agreement reached by warring Beaver and Cree tribes near here, this historic spot was also the base from which Alexander Mackenzie pushed off up the river and made his first European crossing of North America in 1793. Since the 1893 Chicago Exposition when wheat grown here was judged best in the world, this has been a thriving agricultural area.

Right: **Sunset over the Peace River**

Fossil dinosaur tracks have been found on its banks, and over the eons, this great 1923 kilometre river has cut a deep valley into the northern plains. A view near the town of Peace River reveals the water as the highway it once was, carrying fur traders and then settlers into this remote land. The river's headwaters are found to the west in the distant Rocky Mountains of British Columbia.

Waves of Clouds on Island Lake

Lakes are ubiquitous in northeastern Alberta, but only a few are well known or developed for recreation as provincial parks. Every town has its local fishing and swimming holes. This quiet lake is a favourite for the folks of nearby Smoky Lake.

Right: **Cross Lake Provincial Park**

A 2078 hectare park near Athabasca offers a first taste of the boreal forest to visitors from the south. Shaped like a cross, this body of water is officially named Steele Lake. Large northern pike lurk in the lake, while moose, black bears, and summer warblers live along its forested shores.

Sunset north of Cold Lake

Can you hear the loons?

Left: **Sleigh Ride near St. Paul**

Dashing through the snow, at 25 below, these northerners know the trick to enjoying winter. They dress for it. Despite what the thermometer may read, the dry cold lacks the bone-chilling impact of more humid winter climates. On a calm, sunny day, it's simply invigorating.

Black Bear

Every visitor to the north wants to see a bear. However, since we have learned to cut off their sources of human food, bears don't want to see us. Nonetheless, they can often be seen when feeding along green roadsides and in open meadows during spring and early summer. Watch for them close to the security of the forests.

Right: **Great Gray Owl**

Returning to its young with a freshly caught vole, this huge bird is the largest owl in North America. It hunts by day—using the perch-then-pounce technique—over muskegs, wet meadows, and forest edges. An exceptionally tame bird when encountered, it was often shot by unthinking trappers and hunters until its plight was championed by Alberta naturalist Al Oeming in the 1950s.

Devonshire Beach, Lesser Slave Lake Provincial Park

Wolf tracks sometimes mark the white sand here, part of 8 kilometres of beaches on the east end of this 84 kilometre long lake. In the summer, the shores are busy with swimmers and sunners. Just south of the park is the city of Slave Lake and the beginning of settlement; to the north is a vast forest, sprinkled with First Nation villages, logging camps, and fishing lodges.

Left: **Old-growth Boreal Forest, Sir Winston Churchill Provincial Park**

On an island in Lac La Biche, this ancient forest of giant balsam fir, spruce, and paper birch has been spared from fire for 350 years—a rare history in a land of dry, lightning-sparked summers. Such forests, with their dead and dying trees, fallen logs, and lush understory provide a unique habitat for wildlife. Over 200 species of birds have been seen in the park and the shallow lake around it, a bird sanctuary since 1920.

Fly-in Fishing at Grist Lake, North of Cold Lake

Angler's dreams come true on the thousands of lakes in the North. Many are specially managed Trophy Lakes which produce exceptionally large lake trout, walleye, and northern pike. Though roads are pushing ever farther into the wilderness, aircraft are still the only way to get to many of these fantastic fishing holes.

Left: **Lac La Biche Mission Historic Site**

Lac La Biche, on a major portage between the North Saskatchewan and Athabasca Rivers, was a strategic location for a fur trade post. By 1800 both the Hudson's Bay Company and the rival North West Company had established forts here. Missionary Oblates followed in 1844, and in 1853 they founded the Mission of Notre Dame des Victoires. These pioneers operated Alberta's first sawmill and printing press. As well, they grew the first commercial wheat crop, recreated in the foreground. Today the location is both a provincial and national historic site.

Another Alberta Sunset